Carolyn Kyle
presents

Stained Glass
by Candlelight

Ken Bird

CKE Publications
Olympia, Washington

Acknowledgements

This book is for John, a very special friend and mentor.

Special thanks to Shannon Galbreath for her technical photographs.
Also to Kay, Vicki, Cindy, Bev, and Debbie for being my test class for this concept.
And to my staff who encourage me, put up with me, and offer great criticism,
I say "Thank You...."

Ken T. Bird

> Ken Bird owns Dakota Stained Glass and Frame Co. in Sioux Falls, South Dakota.
> He has been teaching and producing stained glass for the past twenty years.
> During this time he has also been involved in the gift industry, the fabric and
> needlecraft markets, and the art and framing industries. This is his first book.

Book Production: Carolyn Kyle, Eldisa Kljucanin
Photography: Chuck Berets, Shannon Galbreath
Printed in the U.S.A. by ESP Printing, Kent, WA

Copyright © CKE Publications, 1998.
Copyright © Ken Bird, 1998. Covers all actual designs used in this publication.

ISBN 0-935133-70-4

Distribution

CKE PUBLICATIONS
2840 Black Lake Blvd., Suite E
Olympia, WA 98512-6197
USA
Tel: (360) 352-4427
FAX: 360-943-3978
E-mail: CKEPUBS@AOL.COM

CKE PUBLICATIONS EUROPE
Tichelbrink 68
D-32584 Loehne
Germany
Telefon: 05731-83307
FAX: 05731-82840

 Call CKE at 1-800-428-7402 to ask for a free catalog of our books and patterns, also for information about our pattern enlargement service.

Introduction

Welcome to the world of stained glass by candlelight; a new concept, making candle rings and candle screens with the elegance of a Tiffany lamp. The candle flickers, the glass glows, these are gorgeous!

As with most Tiffany-style designs, these projects contain quite a few pieces. Added pieces yield added beauty, but here they are also used to facilitate the curved surface of the cylinder, and to maintain line flow around the circle. As the author tells his students, "Many pieces do not make the pattern more complex, they just increase the amount of time required to do the project! You can make one 150-piece project or five 30-piece projects, none are harder than the other." We hope that you will follow this philosophy. With it, you have opened the doors to making Tiffany-like creations that will be enjoyed and treasured for years to come.

Use a glass votive candle holder inside your finished project, making sure it does not touch the stained glass. It is also important to never leave a burning candle unattended. Avoid drafts to discourage uneven burning of the candle.

If the candle ring or screen will be used as a light source, fairly wispy or transparent glass must be used. However, if the objective of the candle is strictly for mood and atmosphere, using the beautiful multi-colored art glasses (as shown in this book's color photos) will give richness and beauty to the project. In all situations, avoid using very dense glass because the candlelight will not be seen through it.

Basic Supplies

1. 14" of PVC pipe in diameter called for in the pattern
2. Three photocopies of the pattern
3. Clear contact paper
4. Masking tape
5. Tacky wax or similar solid adhesive material, available from stained glass store.
6. 3/16", 7/32", and 1/4" copper foil
7. Soy release solvent or kerosene
8. 20 gauge wire
9. Variety of glass, mirror
10. Mirror protector
11. Solder (60/40 is recommended)
12. Stained glass tools

2", 3", and 4" PVC Pipe

Preparing the PVC pipe candle ring mold

PVC pipe, commonly used in plumbing, is an ideal mold material for cylindrical glasswork. It is lightweight, not damaged by solder, and holds its shape. It is available from hardware stores, building material centers, or anywhere that plumbing supplies are sold.

Look on the pattern you have chosen to find the correct diameter of PVC pipe to buy. (This will be 2, 3, or 4 inches.) Use a hacksaw to cut your pipe mold 12 to 14 inches long, which is purposely longer than the actual pattern height.

Preparing the candle ring pattern

1. Make three photocopies of the pattern. One will be cut up for pattern pieces, one will be wrapped around the pipe, and one will be kept as a flat layout guide to keep individual pattern and glass pieces organized.

2. Use *regular scissors* to cut a single line between each of the pattern pieces. Pattern shears should not be used, because the curve of the cylinder will create spaces wide enough to accommodate the foil and solder.

3. On the copy of the pattern that will be wrapped around the pipe, leave 1" of blank paper above and below the pattern. Carefully cut one side exactly to the pattern's edge, but leave extra paper attached on the other side.

Constructing the candle ring

Follow these basic instructions for all 2", 3", and 4" diameter PVC pipe candle rings.

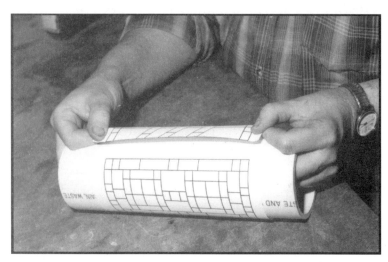

The pattern is wrapped around the pipe with the design's cut edge overlapping the paper and meeting the other end of the design.

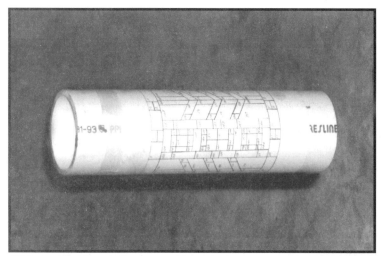

After covering the design area with contact paper, masking tape is used to fasten the top edge of the paper to the pipe

Below: The candle ring is held level and flat while soldering.

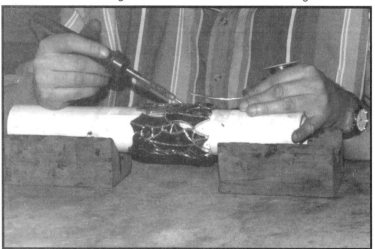

1. Wrap the pattern around the middle of the pipe, ending with the cut pattern edge, which will just meet the uncut end of the pattern. Secure by taping paper to paper, do not tape pattern to pipe. This should form a continuous ring of the pattern design around the pipe. However, size variations of up to 1/8" do occur in the PVC pipe. If a pattern gap or overlap occurs, simply adapt the glass pieces later at one end, through cutting or grozing, to make up for this problem.

2. Cut a piece of clear contact paper one inch shorter than the height of the wrapped paper and one inch longer than the pattern's circumference. Wrap around the pattern, being careful that no contact paper touches the pipe, overlapping ends where they meet. The entire design area must be covered by the contact paper, but none should touch the pipe.

3. Tape the pattern to the pipe along the top edge of the paper only. This is the only place that should be attached to the pipe.

4. Using the pattern pieces and flat layout sheet for reference, cut and groze all glass pieces. Clean each piece, wrap with foil, and place on layout sheet ready to be attached to the pattern cylinder. Leave any pattern shaded spaces open, as indicated on the pattern.

5. Use wooden blocks with a 90° notch removed (see photo) or use pads of old towels, etc., to prop up each end of the cylinder equally. This will elevate the glass above the worktable, allow for easy rotation, and provide a level surface for soldering.

6. Use tacky wax to stick each glass piece in place on the pattern cylinder. The wax can be used as tiny balls, stuck onto the back of the glass and then pressed onto the cylinder, or it can be melted in a cool oven and then applied to the back of the glass with a natural bristle brush. Continue until all glass pieces are attached around the cylinder, leaving any shaded spaces open.

7. Solder the entire outside of the candle ring, rotating the pipe as needed to maintain a flat, level surface. The author recommends using a 1/8" tip for adequate heat with good control to discourage solder from running through the seams.

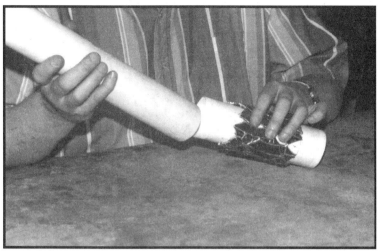

The pattern and candle ring are carefully removed from the PVC pipe.

8. Remove the masking tape from around the top edge of the pattern.

9. Gently tap the bottom of the pipe on the worktable until the candle ring and pattern start to slide down the pipe, then pull to remove.

10. Carefully peel the contact-covered pattern away from the inside and slide it out one end.

11. Remove excess tacky wax from the inside with an old toothbrush and soy release solvent or warm kerosene.

12. Laying the candle ring flat on the worktable, solder the inside, working from each end.

13. Reinforce and finish the top and bottom of the candle ring by burying a continuous length of 20 gauge wire along each edge. 20 gauge wire will bend easily around all intricate curves and angles. A 1/8" solder tip will facilitate this procedure.

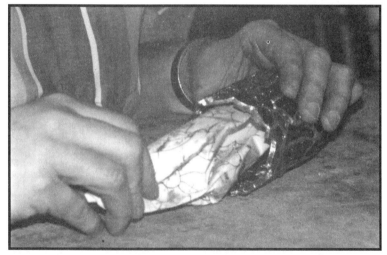

The contact-covered pattern is peeled away from the candle ring.

Below: the inside of the candle ring is soldered.

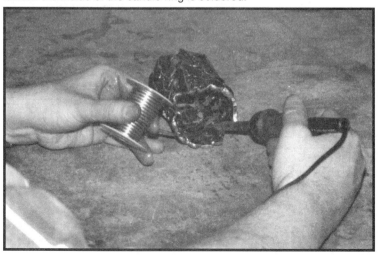

A word about illumination

If you would like a higher amount of illumination than a candle flame will provide, wiring for electricity becomes an option. The small and medium rings can easily be wired with the socket and cord sets that are commonly available from stained glass stores, substituting a 7 wt. bulb for the 4 wt. bulb. When building the ring, leave an open space in the bottom edge to allow for the thickness of the cord.

The medium and large rings will fit on some of the Bradley Base light fixtures, allowing you to wire with a ceramic socket and use a 40 wt. bulb as the light source.

Whether illuminated by candle or light bulb, the light will be magnified if the candle ring is set on a piece of mirror, a beveled mirror, or a mirror trivet. The trivets come in round, square, or hexagon shapes and can be purchased at most major gift stores.

Field Flower Candle Ring

Build on 2″ diameter PVC pipe

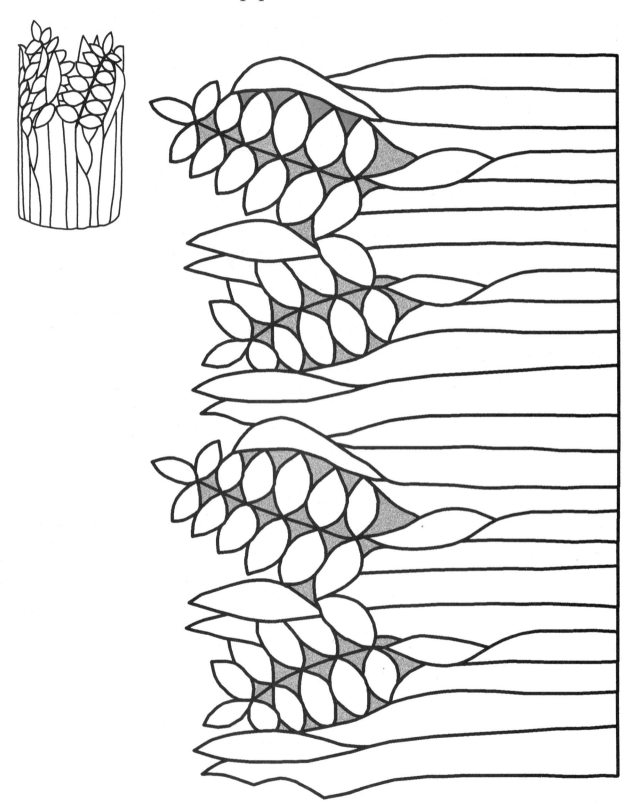

Make the flower stems by laying 12 gauge copper wire between petals as shown on the pattern. Do not attempt to run wire around the top, simply build up the edge with solder.

 =Open Space

Tulip Candle Ring
Build on 2″ diameter PVC pipe

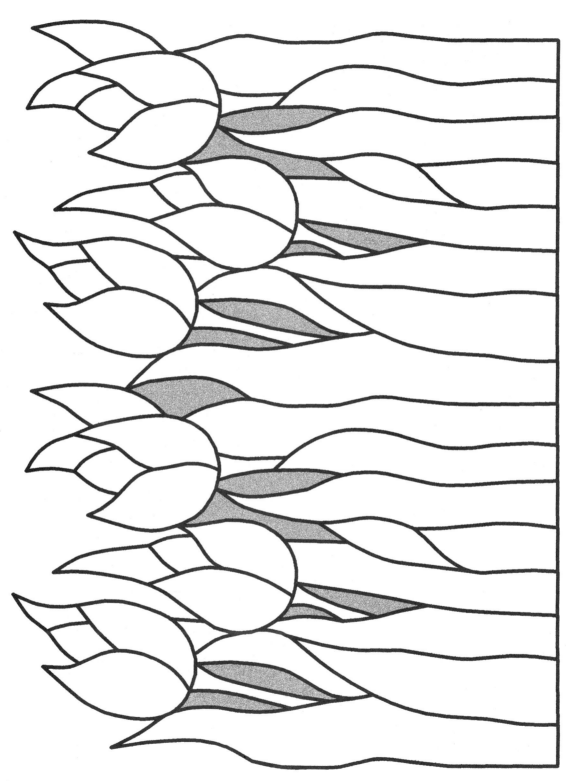

Follow basic candle ring instructions
on pages 3 to 5 for all candle rings.

 = Open Space

Ribbons n' Bows Candle Ring

Build on 3″ diameter PVC pipe

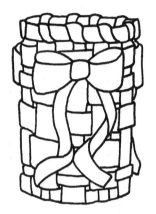

Follow basic candle ring instructions on pages 3 to 5.

Solder the outer edges of the bow pieces and the ends of the ribbons so that they purposely protrude from the cylinder. This will create a three-dimensional effect and allow light to gleam through the openings.

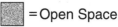 = Open Space

Rose Candle Ring

Build on 3" diameter PVC pipe

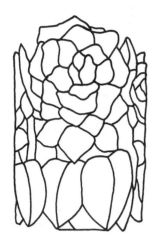

Follow the basic candle ring
instructions on pages 3 to 5.

 = Open Space

Daffodil Candle Ring

Build on 3″ diameter PVC pipe

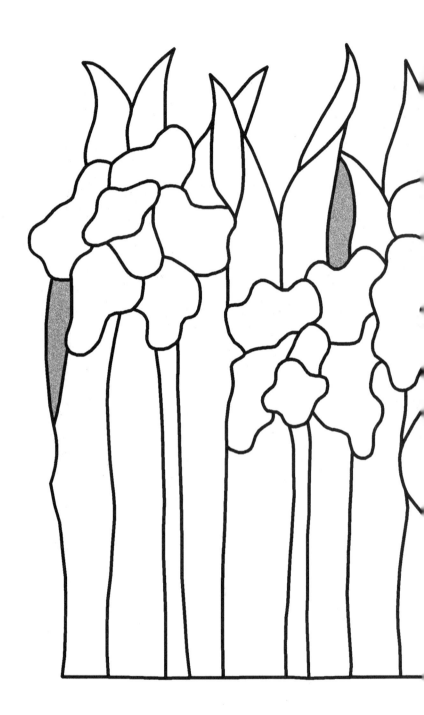

Follow the basic candle ring
instructions on pages 3 to 5.

 = Open Space

Prairie Candle Ring

Build on 3" diameter PVC pipe

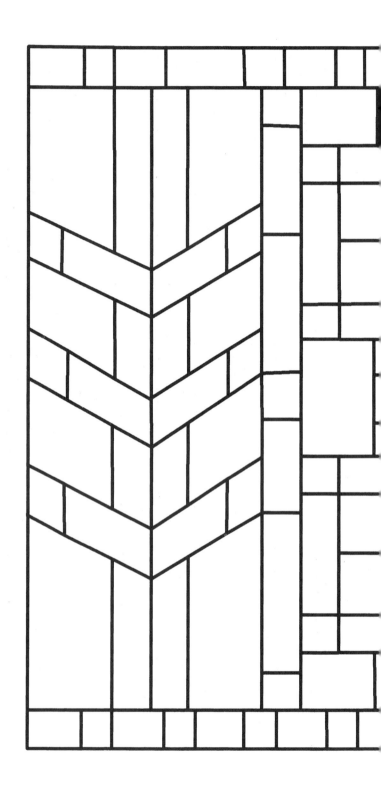

Follow basic candle ring instructions on pages 3 to 5.

Variation: For a more open prairie candle ring, eliminate some of the pieces in a logical repetition, creating open spaces that will allow the candlelight to flicker through.

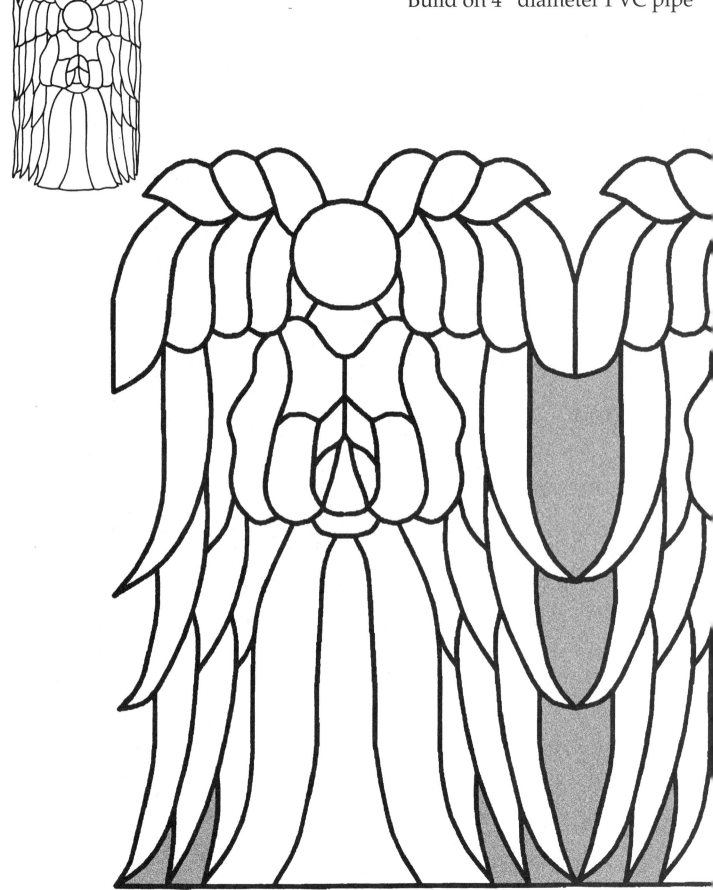

Angel Candle Ring

Build on 4″ diameter PVC pipe

presents

Stained Glass by Candlelight
Addendum

Oops!! Mistakes do happen....

Since the printing of this book, it has been discovered that the four inch candle ring patterns on pages 16 through 25 are not the correct size.

When making any of the four inch candle rings, please use the full-size patterns contained in this addendum, not the patterns on pages 16 through 25.

All the other patterns in this book are correct.

Any questions?

Just call CKE at 360-352-4427 or 1-800-428-7402

We're always happy to assist.

Design and instructions are complete on each piece of paper. Separate to use.

Angel Candle Ring
Build on 4" diameter PVC pipe

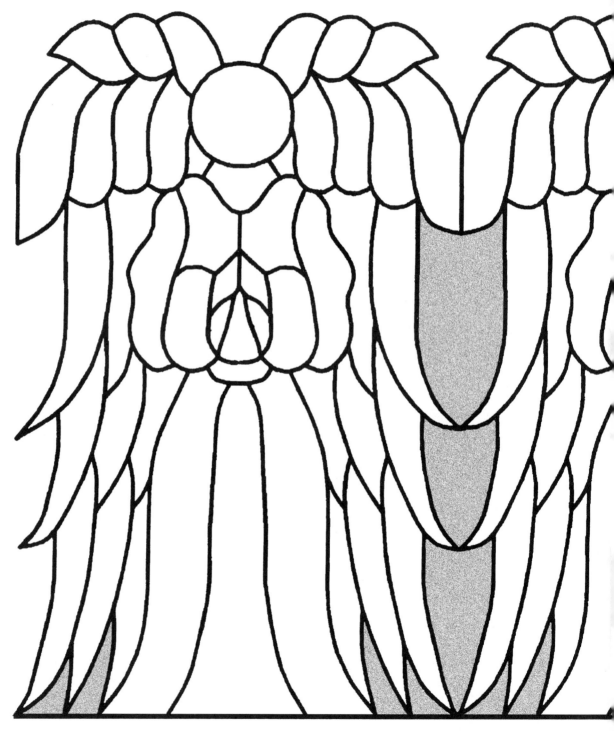

2

= Open Space

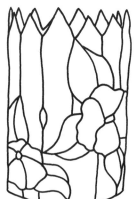

Picket Fence Candle Ring
Build on 4" diameter PVC pipe

Hummingbird Candle Ring Build on 4" diameter PVC pipe

= Open Space

Follow the basic candle ring instructions on pages 3 to 5.
Bird eyes: Drop a bead of solder where the lines on each
head intersect.

Tulip Candle Ring

Build on 4" diameter PVC pip

 = Open Space

9

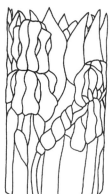

Iris Candle Ring
Build on 4" diameter PVC pipe

Follow basic candle ring instructions on pages 3 to 5.

Round 35 mm faceted jewels can be used for the angels' heads. White or light blue wispy iridescent glass, as well as clear iridescent glass, would be ideal for these lovely beings.

 = Open Space

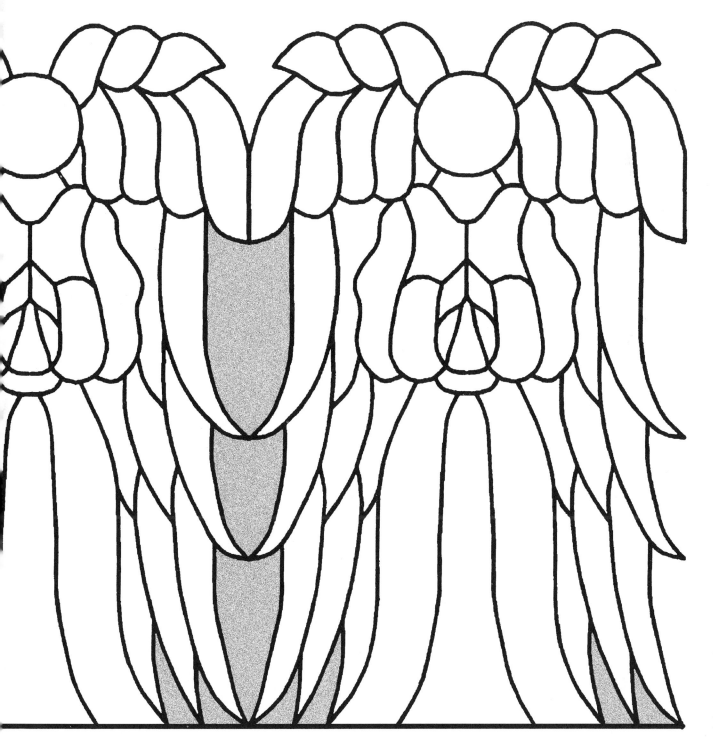

CKE Publications
Olympia, Washington

Follow basic candle ring instructions on pages 3 to 5.

Round 35 mm faceted jewels can be used for the angels' heads. White or light blue wispy iridescent glass, as well as clear iridescent glass, would be ideal for these lovely beings.

 = Open Space

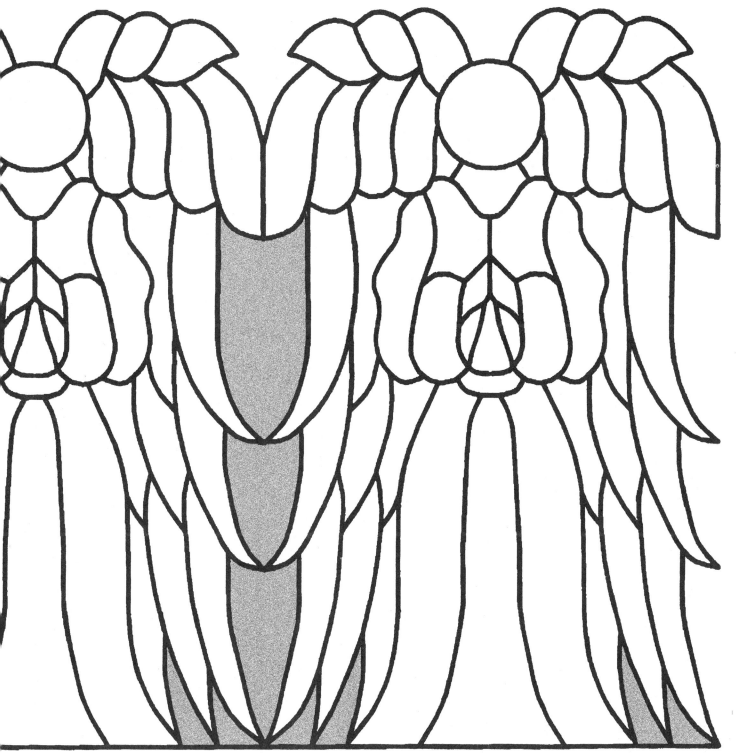

Iris Candle Ring
Build on 4″ diameter PVC pipe

Follow the basic candle ring instructions on pages 3 to 5.

 =Open Space

19

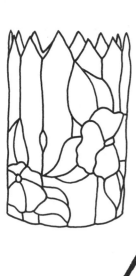

Picket Fence Candle Ring
Build on 4″ diameter PVC pipe

Follow the basic candle ring
instructions on pages 3 to 5.

 = Open Space

Tulip Candle Ring

Build on 4" diameter PVC pipe

Follow the basic candle ring instructions on pages 3 to 5.

= Open Space

Hummingbird Candle Ring

Build on 4″ diameter PVC pipe

= Open Space

Follow the basic candle ring instructions on pages 3 to 5.
Bird eyes: Drop a bead of solder where the lines on each head intersect.

25

Holly Candle Ring
Build on 2″ diameter PVC pipe

Follow the basic candle ring instructions on pages 3 to 5. Red glass nuggets can be used for realistic holly berries.

= Open Space

Candle Screen Base Pattern

Use for all candle screens, pages 28 through 32.

Cut along *outside edge* of black line.

Constructing a candle screen

Each candle screen is made of a center panel, two side panels, and a mirror base. To illuminate the candle screen, a votive candle in a glass votive cup is placed on the mirror. These look great on shelves or tables, with only the curved front of the screen showing. The candle, hidden, softly glows, illuminating the glass from behind.

As with the candle rings, choose glass with colorful streaks and textures, but avoid dense opalescent glass, since candlelight will not show through. Follow the instructions below to make any of the screen patterns on pages 28 through 32, using the base pattern on the opposite page for each screen.

1. Make two photocopies of the pattern, one for pattern pieces and one for a layout sheet. To make pattern pieces, use *regular scissors* to cut the outside of the black line around each panel and around a copy of the base pattern. *Use copper foil shears to cut apart all the inside lines on the three panels.*

2. Cut base piece from double strength (1/8") mirror. Seal mirror edges with silver protector. Wrap mirror edge with 1/4" copper foil.

3. Cut all glass pieces, fit, then wrap with 3/16" or 7/32" copper foil.

4. Lay glass pieces out on the layout sheet, then check. All outside lines must be straight and must not extend beyond the pattern. Also check to see that all glass pieces line up properly from one panel to another.

5. Solder each of the three panels separately, turn over and solder the back sides. Do not build up solder on the outside panel edges.

6. Place the middle panel on the mirror with the bottom inside edge of the panel sitting on the top outside edge of the mirror base. Tack-solder.

7. Tack-solder the side panels in place, with their bottom inside edges touching the inside edges of the middle panel and the top outside edge of the mirror. Make any adjustments necessary, then completely solder all four pieces together, inside and outside.

8. Beginning at one end of the base edge, bury a continuous strand of 20 gauge copper wire around the entire outside edge of the three joined panels and then around the base until back to where the wire started. This will produce a good, solid candle screen.

Three upright pieces and base are foiled and soldered.

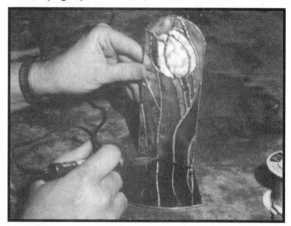

Center piece is tacked to base.

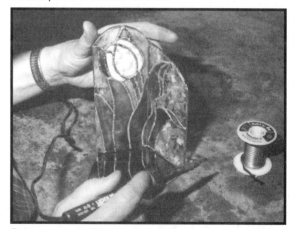

Sides are tacked in place, then entire piece is soldered.

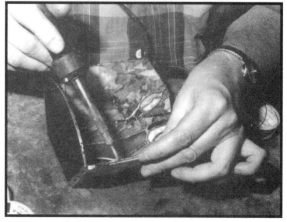

20 gauge wire is buried around entire perimeter.

27

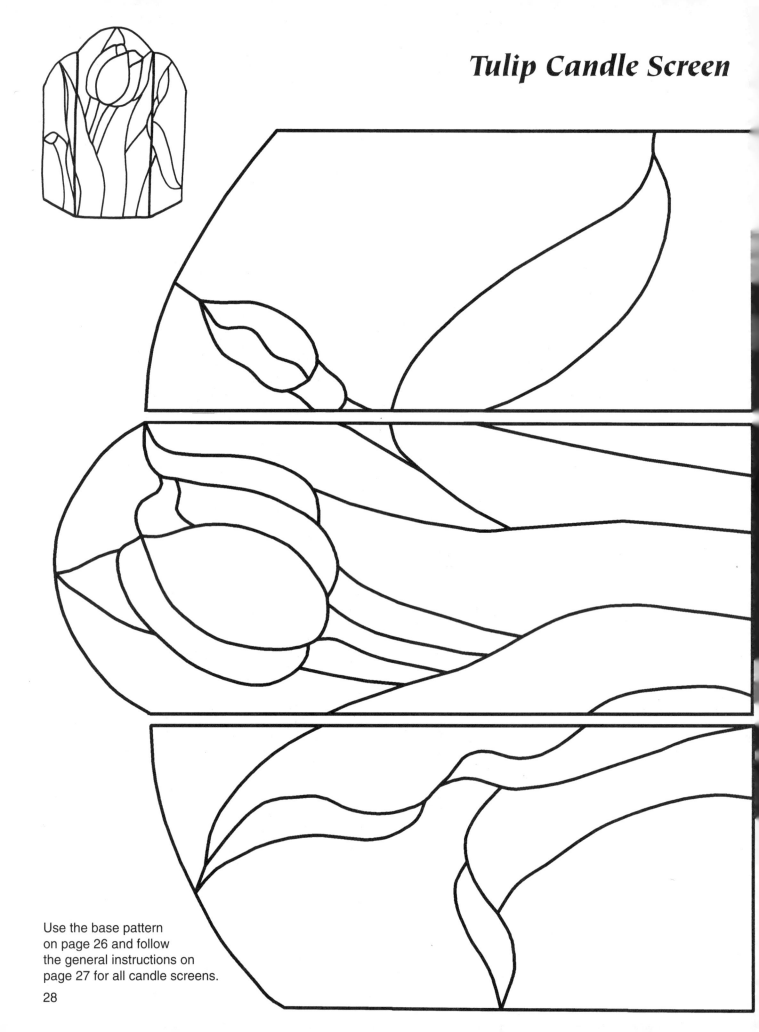

Tulip Candle Screen

Use the base pattern
on page 26 and follow
the general instructions on
page 27 for all candle screens.

Lily Candle Screen

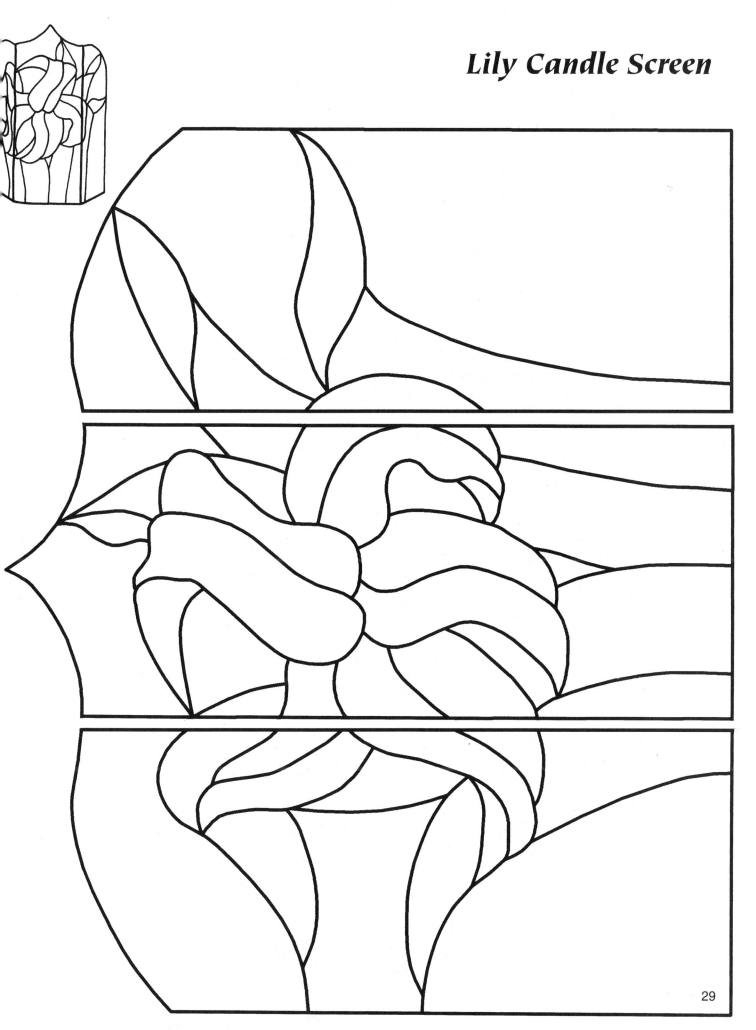

29

Ribbon & Rose Candle Screen

Use the base pattern
on page 26 and follow
the general instructions on
page 27 for all candle screens.

Angel Candle Screen

A round 25mm faceted jewel can be used for the angel's head.

=Open Space

Poinsettia Candle Screen

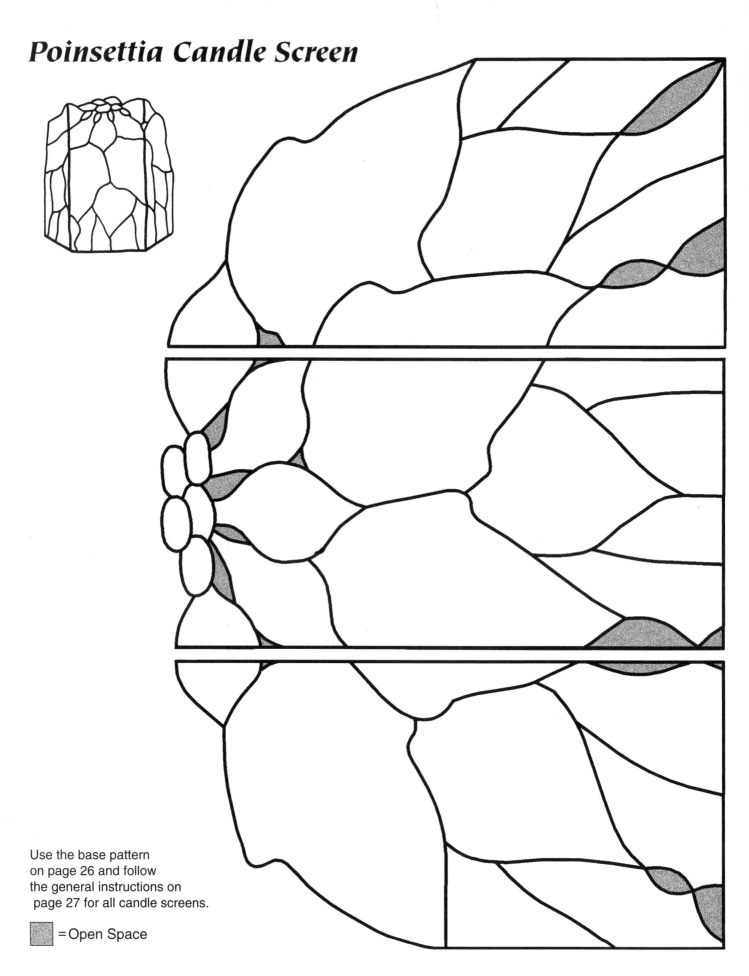

Use the base pattern
on page 26 and follow
the general instructions on
page 27 for all candle screens.

= Open Space